BRAVER
BY THE DAY

A JOURNAL FOR
FINDING YOUR VOICE
AND LIVING BOLDLY

EVA OLSEN

CASTLE POINT BOOKS
NEW YORK

www.castlepointbooks.com

The Castle Point Books trademark is owned by Castle Point Publishing, LLC.
Castle Point books are published and distributed by St. Martin's Press.

ISBN 978-1-250-27209-6 (trade paperback)

Special thanks to Therese Walsh

Our books may be purchased in bulk for promotional, educational, or business use.
Please contact your local bookseller or the Macmillan Corporate and Premium
Sales Department at 1-800-221-7945, extension 5442, or by email
at MacmillanSpecialMarkets@macmillan.com.

First Edition: 2020

10 9 8 7 6 5 4 3 2 1

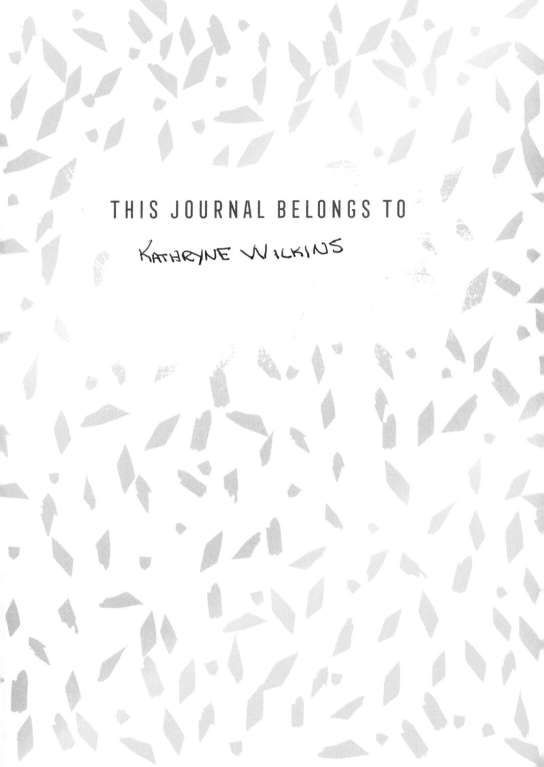

THIS JOURNAL BELONGS TO

Kathryne Wilkins

LIFE SHRINKS OR EXPANDS IN PROPORTION TO ONE'S COURAGE.

ANAÏS NIN

INTRODUCTION

WE ALL DESERVE A PLACE AT THE TABLE, A VOICE, AND A CHANCE TO
LIVE WITH BOLD INTENTIONS. THIS IS YOURS.

If this journal called to you, you're probably tired of letting your self-
consciousness steer you down the safest path. You've gotten alarmingly
good at stepping back and letting others surge ahead. You have a Ph.D.
in self-restraint, a black belt in people-pleasing, and a knack for lassoing
your ambitions before they wander too far—but there's another way to
live, and the time to try it is now.

Braver by the Day is a companion journal for challenging your self-
imposed limitations and making your mark on the world using all the
strengths in your arsenal. Every day is a good day to aim higher and figure
out what, exactly, is holding you back. We all know people who fight for
what they want and take no prisoners. Imagine the empowerment of
adopting their strategies as your own and living just a little bit (or even a
whole lot) larger. Use the prompts in this journal to get out of your own
way, to find the courage and confidence to take risks, and to head bravely
in the direction of the life you want.

SUCCESS

IS LIKING YOURSELF,
LIKING WHAT YOU DO,
AND LIKING
HOW YOU DO IT.

MAYA ANGELOU

EVERYONE, YOU INCLUDED, HAS WHAT IT TAKES TO BE BRAVE. Use this page to assure yourself that the ingredients are there—ready to be called upon. Describe an environment or situation where you become the boldest version of yourself. Where or when do you cease to second guess yourself and allow your instincts to take the lead?

What might this tell you about yourself and your potential?

DON'T LET OTHERS MAKE YOU FEEL SMALL. Who do you find most intimidating? It can be a specific person or a type of person. What is the root of this feeling, if you had to guess?

How might this person actually have a reason to be intimidated by you? What secret weapon do you have that you haven't used?

FEARS ARE EDUCATED INTO US, AND CAN, IF WE WISH, BE EDUCATED OUT.

KARL AUGUSTUS MENNINGER

REFUSE TO BACK DOWN. When have you talked yourself out of doing something that was scary? How did you justify backing down from a situation?

Be ready the next time this happens so you can get out of your own way. Trim your thoughts down to those that are actually helpful and productive. The rest of your narrative is probably springing from fear and doubt. Get better at silencing the wrong voices so you can hear the right ones.

THE MOST EFFECTIVE WAY TO DO IT, IS TO DO IT.

AMELIA EARHART

MAKE YOUR VOICE HEARD. Reflect on the last time you were in a social or professional setting and you held back in a way that you later regretted. What made you stifle your voice? Where do you think you learned this habit?

What did you accomplish by being unheard? What might you have accomplished if you'd stepped up and spoken up?

I DON'T REGRET
THE THINGS I'VE DONE,
I REGRET
THE THINGS
I DIDN'T DO
WHEN I HAD THE CHANCE.

UNKNOWN

THINK LIKE A QUEEN. A QUEEN IS NOT AFRAID TO FAIL. FAILURE IS ANOTHER STEPPING STONE TO GREATNESS.

OPRAH WINFREY

BE AS STRONG AS YOU HOPE TO BE. Pretending to be brave is one of the simplest ways to become braver. The next time you feel panicked or fearful, visualize the behavior of the strongest person you know. What would this person do in that situation? Channel their energy and proceed as if you were them. Describe a situation where this exercise would be helpful.

BUILD YOUR OWN DREAMS,

OR SOMEONE ELSE WILL HIRE YOU TO BUILD THEIRS.

FARRAH GRAY

GET IT. What is one thing you want in your life or career, but haven't managed to accomplish? Why do you think you have yet to accomplish it?

DON'T GET
TOO COMFORTABLE
WITH WHO YOU ARE
AT ANY GIVEN TIME—
YOU MAY MISS THE
OPPORTUNITY TO BECOME
WHO YOU WANT TO BE.

JON BON JOVI

REFLECT ON your list of personal goals, and divide them into
two lists below:

MY PERSONAL GOALS   GOALS I'VE SET TO PLEASE OTHERS

Cast off the vision others have for you and go for yours.

CONSIDER YOUR DREAMS AND GOALS from the last exercise. Now ask yourself why you want those things, and write those answers below.

Now ask again of your above answers: Why? Ask and answer this question until you cannot dig any deeper; until your motivations touch something personal and perhaps surprising. Circle those answers.

HE WHO HAS
A WHY TO LIVE
CAN BEAR
ALMOST
ANY HOW.

FRIEDRICH NIETZSCHE

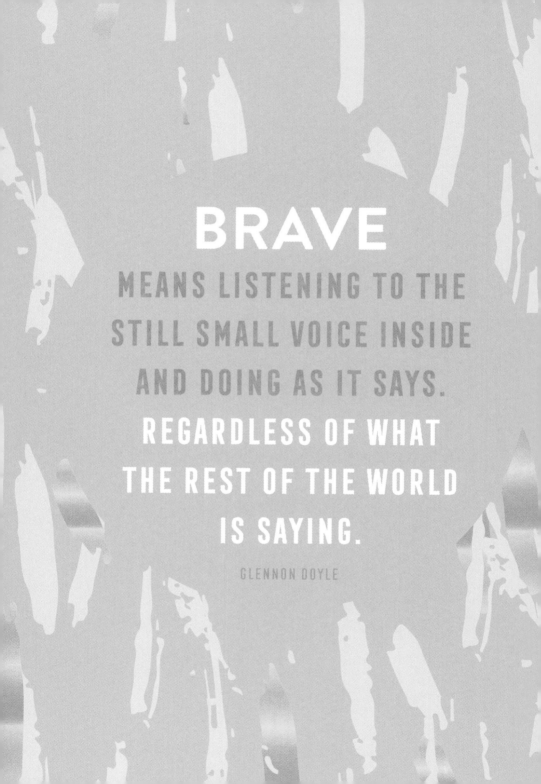

BRAVE

MEANS LISTENING TO THE
STILL SMALL VOICE INSIDE
AND DOING AS IT SAYS.

REGARDLESS OF WHAT
THE REST OF THE WORLD
IS SAYING.

GLENNON DOYLE

THERE IS A LOT OF NOISE IN THIS WORLD, and much of it may whisper the wrong things in your ear. Maybe these whispers make you doubt yourself because of your gender, your race, your sexual orientation, your age, or your background. They can't blunt your dreams and your bravery if you don't let them, so don't let them.

Find your voice as you read this mantra:

ONLY I KNOW WHAT I'M TRULY CAPABLE OF, AND I KNOW I CAN DO THIS. JUST WATCH ME.

Write more mantras below in your own words.

PAST FAILURES are not indications of future failure. They're signs that you're getting closer to your goal.

Have you ever given up on something after trying only once, and regretted that choice? Why do you think you gave up? If you could go back in time and counsel your past self, what would you say? What would you like to tell your future self, if she, too, wants to give up on something important to you?

I HAVE
NOT FAILED.
I'VE JUST FOUND
10,000 WAYS THAT
WON'T WORK.

THOMAS EDISON

LIFE IS VERY INTERESTING...
IN THE END,
SOME OF YOUR
GREATEST PAINS
BECOME YOUR
GREATEST STRENGTHS.

DREW BARRYMORE

IT'S HARD FOR PEOPLE who are used to critiquing themselves to look in the mirror and acknowledge their strengths. What do you do well that others may find difficult? What struggles did you have that morphed into strengths? Name those strengths here. Capitalize every letter. Be loud, and be proud.

BEING BRAVE takes practice, which means putting yourself out there a lot, and yes, failing. One of the hardest things to combat when you fail is a sense of tattered pride.

Write out something that you are genuinely proud to have accomplished. What trials did you face on the way to attaining it?

How different might things have been if you'd made other choices, or chose not to act? Fill in the following:

"I'M SO GLAD THAT ....
...."

"I WILL NEVER REGRET ....
...."

"I NEVER KNEW THAT I HAD IT IN ME TO...
...."

TAKE CHANCES, MAKE MISTAKES. YOU HAVE TO FAIL IN ORDER TO PRACTICE BEING BRAVE.

MARY TYLER MOORE

FEW EXPERIENCES ARE
MORE SATISFYING THAN
BECOMING SOMEONE
WE ALWAYS IMAGINED
WE COULD BE.

GINA GREENLEE

CONSIDER YOUR CHILDHOOD DREAMS. What did you believe you might do? When you look at your life through the eyes of your younger self, what do you see?

If you could go back in time and give your child-self one piece of advice to help her succeed, what would you say? Do you still need this advice today?

YOUR ADVENTURE INTO BRAVERY will reveal new things about yourself—good things. Sometimes hidden sides of yourself end up lighting the way. What sides of you have emerged as you've grown into yourself? What new side(s) of yourself are you ready to show the world?

MAKE THE MOST
OF YOURSELF BY
FANNING THE TINY,
INNER SPARKS
OF POSSIBILITY
INTO FLAMES OF
ACHIEVEMENT.

GOLDA MEIR

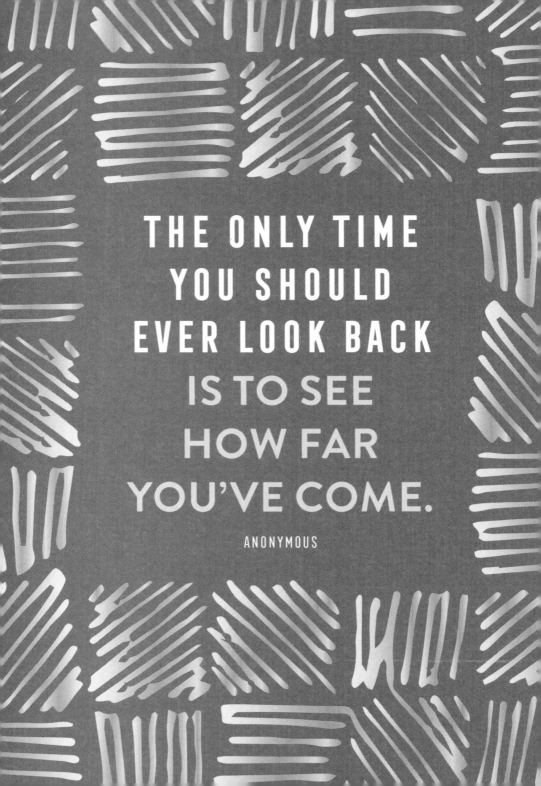

THE ONLY TIME
YOU SHOULD
EVER LOOK BACK
IS TO SEE
HOW FAR
YOU'VE COME.

ANONYMOUS

AS YOU JOURNEY TOWARD YOUR GOALS, consider rewarding yourself for milestones as you reach them. These rewards can fuel you with a conscious awareness of your own significant progress, which in turn can inspire more significant progress.

Consider the milestones you've reached so far and look back to admire them. How might you celebrate them today or in the future?

LEARN TO BUILD YOURSELF UP. Become your own best advocate. Being able to battle back negative chatter and bring on the affirmations is one part of this. Take some time now to create two columns. Add the negative chatter you use against yourself in the left column in bullet-point form. Directly next to each of those points, in the right column, add your positive push-back.

NEGATIVE CHATTER   POSITIVE PUSH-BACK

In this battle between your most negative and positive selves, your positive self must prevail. Be sure that it does.

TALK TO YOURSELF
LIKE A TRUSTED FRIEND
AND REFUSE TO BELIEVE
YOUR UNREALISTIC,
NEGATIVE INNER
MONOLOGUE.

AMY MORIN

I DO MY BEST
BECAUSE I'M
COUNTING ON YOU
COUNTING
ON ME.

MAYA ANGELOU

WELCOME THE HELP OF OTHERS. It can be your greatest advantage. Even the strongest people benefit from having allies—people they can rely on to cheer them on and fuel them up when their gas tanks are empty. And when you're striving toward new goals, when you're working hard to be brave, these voices are even more precious.

Who can you rely upon when you need encouragement or accountability? Is it easy or difficult for you to ask for help from others?

IMAGINE YOUR BRAVE NEW SELF IN THE FUTURE. Goals have been met. You are happier. Could you have stayed in your comfort zone, or do you think you had to step out of it—perhaps by a wide mile—to attain your goals? What might you dare yourself to do today or in the near future to step out of your comfort zone?

TELL ME, WHAT IS IT YOU PLAN TO DO WITH YOUR ONE WILD AND PRECIOUS LIFE?

MARY OLIVER

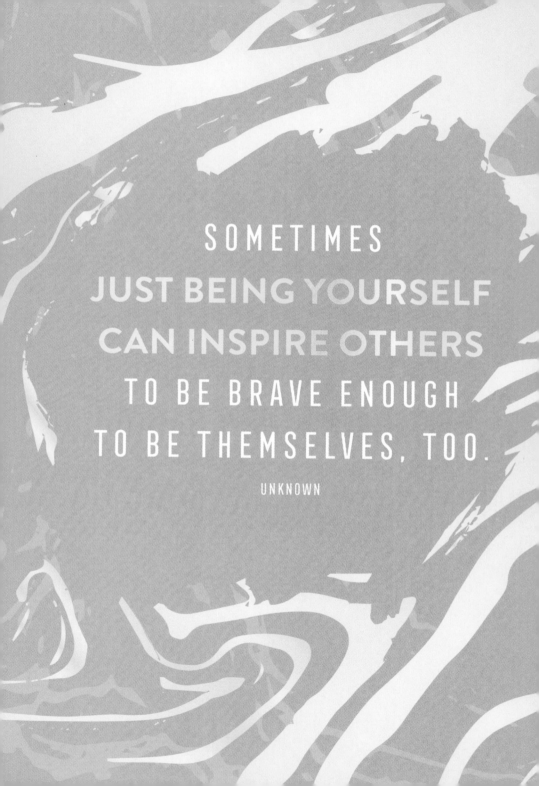

SOMETIMES
JUST BEING YOURSELF
CAN INSPIRE OTHERS
TO BE BRAVE ENOUGH
TO BE THEMSELVES, TOO.

UNKNOWN

OUR GOALS ARE OUR OWN, but that doesn't mean we can't be inspired to meet them with an awareness of who's watching. Sometimes those who are watching are our children or siblings or friends. If you knew you were being studied in order to be emulated, would that change anything about your behavior? Would it change how you spoke about yourself to others? What seeds of bravery do you want to plant in others?

CHOOSE TO BE FLATTERED whenever others feel the need to hold you back. They must think you are a force to be reckoned with. When have others stood in your way? What secret weapon do you have that you haven't used, but that they may see you possess?

Have you allowed someone to stifle your voice or block your progress without realizing it? Write a note below, rescinding that permission and taking back your power.

THERE ARE TWO TYPES
OF PEOPLE WHO WILL
TELL YOU THAT YOU CANNOT
MAKE A DIFFERENCE
IN THIS WORLD:

**THOSE WHO ARE
AFRAID TO TRY AND
THOSE WHO ARE AFRAID
YOU WILL SUCCEED.**

RAY GOFORTH

SOMETIMES what stands between a person and their dreams is the imagined chaos of getting to them. The journey to happiness may be longer than you want. It may end up disrupting your life. It may, at times, make you feel like a stranger to yourself. And so you wait for some imagined ideal moment when things "settle down," even though some part of you may know that ideal moment is unlikely to ever arrive.

Imagine all the change you might make with a small fundamental shift in your life. How might you use disruption to make changes for the better? Make peace with upheaval by listing below all the reasons why the ends justify the means.

IF YOU WANT THE RAINBOW, YOU GOTTA PUT UP WITH THE RAIN.

DOLLY PARTON

COURAGE DOESN'T ALWAYS ROAR.

SOMETIMES COURAGE IS THE LITTLE VOICE AT THE END OF THE DAY THAT SAYS, *I'LL TRY AGAIN TOMORROW.*

MARY ANNE RADMACHER

HOW CONFIDENT ARE YOU IN YOUR SUCCESS? How adaptable are you when difficulties arise? When have you resolved to try again tomorrow, even when you felt like quitting?

Consider a time when you had to deal with a situation and create a solution on the fly. Which skills saw you through that situation, and toward that solution? Can those same skills help you now?

THIS IS YOUR JOURNEY, YOUR LIFE. Don't measure it against anyone else's. Comparisons are a waste of your productive energy. They fuel self-doubt, and doubt can take all the wind out of your sails.

Make comparisons with only one person: yourself. Compare where you are now with where you were a year ago; five years ago. Compare where you are now with where you hope to be a year from now; five years from now, and so on.

DO NOT COMPETE
WITH ANYONE.

SEEK TO EXCEED YOUR
OWN EXPECTATIONS.

LAILAH GIFTY AKITA

FROM A
SMALL SEED A
MIGHTY TRUNK
MAY GROW.

AESCHYLUS

SOMETIMES IT FEELS as though we give too much for too little growth. This may be especially true when you're in the early stages of making changes in service of a goal. Know that what seems like a small change on the outside may have set the stage for more noticeable future evolutions. With time and nurturing conditions, that seed will grow.

Acknowledge something you feel discouraged about—an act that didn't bear as much fruit as you would have liked. Consider how that act, however small, may lead to more change in the future. What can you do to nurture it?

CONSIDER THE LAST TIME YOU WERE TRULY BRAVE. Did you feel bold just after your brave act? What did you do with that bold feeling? If you powered forward and let that feeling lead you to more brave acts, what would those acts be?

With every move you dare to make, you are growing comfortable in the shoes that a brave person must wear as they traverse the territory of their dreams.

WE BECOME JUST
BY PERFORMING JUST ACTIONS,
TEMPERATE BY PERFORMING
TEMPERATE ACTIONS,
BRAVE BY PERFORMING
BRAVE ACTIONS.

ARISTOTLE

IT TAKES A LOT OF COURAGE TO SHOW YOUR DREAMS TO SOMEONE ELSE.

ERMA BOMBECK

LET YOURSELF BE VULNERABLE. Share your goals with someone whose opinion you deeply value. Who do you admire for their unusual ideas or approaches? Create a list of people in your life who have different perspectives. Imagine how your ideas might take on new dimensions if room is made within them for others' points of view.

LET YOUR IMAGINATION LEAD THE WAY. If you're struggling with something, try giving the problems over to your back-burner self. Think about the problem before you take a walk or drive or shower or go to sleep at night. Give your subconscious the opportunity to consider your plight and blaze a trail through it.

What questions do you find hard to face in the light of day? What would you like to ask your sleeping mind in order to better understand yourself?

WHY DOES THE EYE SEE A THING MORE CLEARLY IN DREAMS THAN THE IMAGINATION WHEN AWAKE?

LEONARDO DA VINCI

KNOWLEDGE
IS
POWER.

FRANCIS BACON

GET WHAT YOU NEED. If you don't have it, seek it out. Recognizing that we need more tools to be who we want to be and do what we want to do is in itself an act of bravery. What part of yourself could you train and strengthen in order to grow?

If you had the opportunity to take a class now to build up your confidence, what would that class be? If you were to acquire a mentor who would pass along tips and guide you along on your journey, who would that be?

THINK ABOUT A TIME when you resisted the urge to quit. Why do you think you continued? Was it for a person, a reward, an ideal?

That motivation may still be a part of you. It pulses beneath your surface and says, *Go, go, go, stay in the race.* Can you find it? Can it fuel other aspects of your life?

Protect that fire against all and everything that would harm it.
That is your greatest tool.

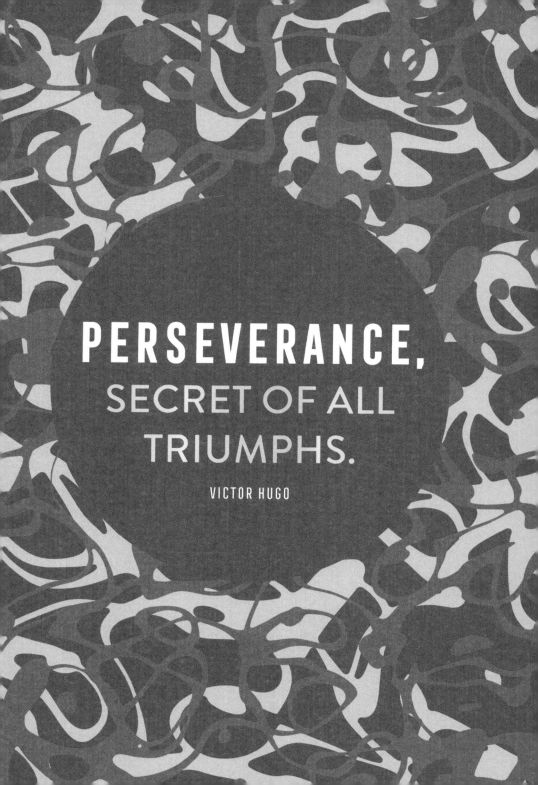

PERSEVERANCE,
SECRET OF ALL
TRIUMPHS.

VICTOR HUGO

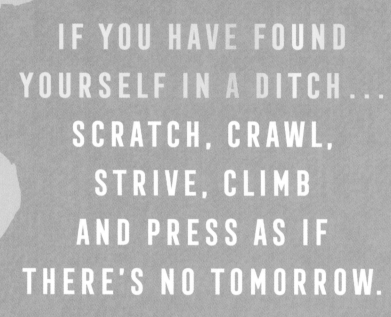

IF YOU HAVE FOUND
YOURSELF IN A DITCH...
SCRATCH, CRAWL,
STRIVE, CLIMB
AND PRESS AS IF
THERE'S NO TOMORROW.

RODNEY WALKER

MAKE REAL CHANGE WHEN YOU NEED IT. If you're in a rut, step back and reassess things from a distance. What empowers this rut? Is this a short- or long-term problem for you?

Do your goals and motivations need another look? Take some time to work through why your tires are spinning, and what you can do to de-rut yourself and get back on the road.

TO ACHIEVE
ANY AIM IN LIFE,
YOU NEED TO PROJECT
THE END RESULT.
THINK OF THE ELATION,
THE SATISFACTION,
THE JOY!

GRACE SPEARE

IMAGINE THAT you are just about to do the very last thing you need to in order to reach your goals. What is that thing? How does it feel to cross that threshold? What is the first thing you will do on the other side of that line?

Create a daily meditation for yourself in which you succeed. Close your eyes. Cycle through it. Your triumphant self is there to witness. Visualize your way to success; visualize the win, and you'll come to see yourself differently, more empowered, braver.

THINK ABOUT YOUR HABITS, the things you do every single day, perhaps even without conscious thought. What new habits can you imagine creating that will lend themselves to succeeding in your goals? Does it require a shift of time, or just a shift in your mindset?

Write out three new potential habits below, and commit to trying them every day for a week, then re-evaluate whether you need new ones.

PROGRESS, NOT PERFECTION, IS WHAT WE SHOULD BE ASKING OF OURSELVES.

JULIA CAMERON

YOU MUST BE ABLE TO WALK FIRMLY ON THE GROUND BEFORE YOU START WALKING ON A TIGHTROPE.

HENRI MATISSE

BABY STEPS can get you where you need to go. Sometimes the magnitude of a goal overwhelms us into stillness. Instead of lamenting the long road ahead, try breaking your goal into manageable chunks. Through the habit of small steps, you will gain confidence in your abilities as you gain ground on your ultimate goal.

Consider one of your overwhelming goals, and break it into small steps below.

FORGET PERFECT. One of the best ways to get out from under the thumb of perfectionism is to realize that "perfect" is a false concept. That's because life is not ultimately controllable, and ideal conditions are either imagined or fleeting.

Do you struggle with perfectionism? Can you see how it might weigh you down? How might your goals change if you asked not for perfection but for the best you can do right now?

PERFECTIONISM
IS THE VOICE
OF THE
OPPRESSOR.

ANNE LAMOTT

WHATEVER YOU CAN DO,
OR DREAM YOU CAN,
BEGIN IT.
BOLDNESS HAS
GENIUS, POWER,
AND MAGIC IN IT.

W. H. MURRAY

SOME OF OUR BRAVEST MOMENTS ARE UNPLANNED. Perhaps something happens that is so counter to our beliefs that we speak or act without much thought. Sometimes we do this in service of someone in need, or in the face of an emergency. We may not even stop to consider how brave we were after the fact, because it was unplanned.

List a few times you stood up to someone or stood strong against something. How did it feel? When have you surprised yourself with your strength?

MODIFY YOUR ENVIRONMENT to make it a place where you matter. Not every environment supports personal growth, so be sure to put yourself in a place where you can be heard. What about your current environment empowers you while you pursue your goals?

What about your current environment makes it challenging for you to pursue your goals? What change can you make to your environment to make it compatible with what you seek in your life?

THE FIRST STEP TOWARD SUCCESS IS TAKEN WHEN YOU REFUSE TO BE A CAPTIVE OF THE ENVIRONMENT IN WHICH YOU FIRST FIND YOURSELF.

MARK CAINE

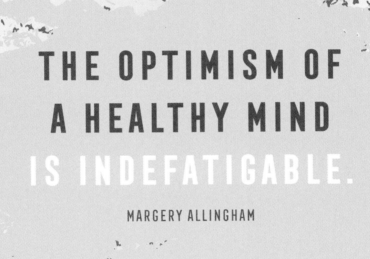

THE OPTIMISM OF A HEALTHY MIND IS INDEFATIGABLE.

MARGERY ALLINGHAM

HEALTHY PEOPLE are, arguably, in the best condition to pursue goals. Since you'll be striving to make changes in other areas of your life as you become braver, consider how your life might be made healthier, too; whether you'd like to improve the health of your body, your mind, or your spirit. Include your healthy goals here, and why you think those goals should be made a priority. How will you go about meeting them?

BE NIMBLE TO GET WHAT YOU WANT. Adaptability is an important tool in the toolbox of success. Successful people often forge new plans when their original plans fall through. Consider some of your most important life goals, and your plans for meeting them. If those plans fail, how will you go about trying another way? Sketch out two or three alternate routes to success.

IF YOUR SHIP DOESN'T COME IN, SWIM OUT TO IT.

JONATHAN WINTERS

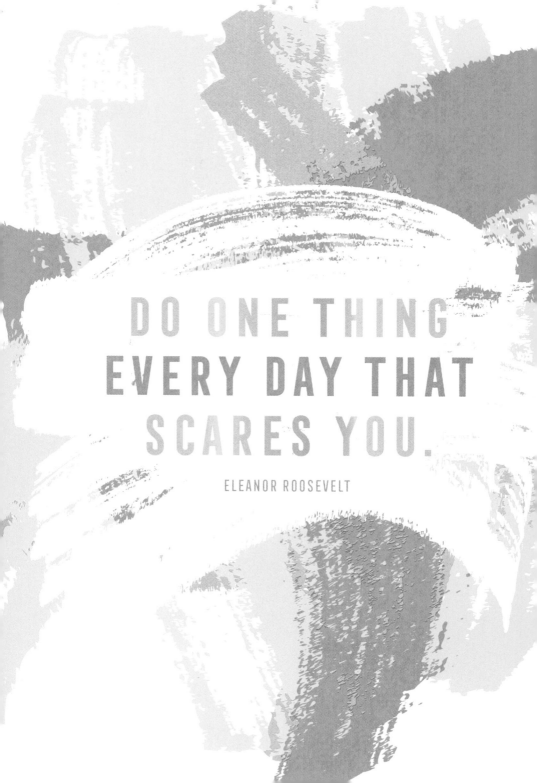

DO ONE THING
EVERY DAY THAT
SCARES YOU.

ELEANOR ROOSEVELT

PRACTICE FEARLESS LIVING AS OFTEN AS YOU CAN. What are you scared to do?

How can you push yourself in ways that can help to expand your capabilities and use new muscles to show yourself, and the world, what you're made of?

IMAGINE THAT YOU ARE YOUR OWN ARCHITECT. Feel the power of knowing whatever comes will be because you took action. Every action builds a new room within the building that is you, and each room represents a significant dream, wish, or goal. Name each room. What is in each one? What are its colors? What hangs on its walls? Which room is your favorite?

Spend a little time in each one, right now, and consider making this exercise a regular part of your daily routine.

LIFE ISN'T ABOUT

FINDING
YOURSELF.

LIFE IS ABOUT

CREATING
YOURSELF.

GEORGE BERNARD SHAW

BRAVE MEANS

YOU'RE ABLE TO ADMIT THAT YOU CARE.

CLAIRE DANES

CARING ABOUT SOMETHING and being vulnerable because of that does not make you weak. In fact, it can inspire your fiercest and most natural shows of strength. What in your life do you care enough about that you're willing to defend it?

Now consider your life goals. Do you care about them as well, or do you care about what attaining those goals might bring you? Can you interlace your goals with the things you care most deeply about?

YOU'RE STRONGER THAN YOU, OR ANYONE ELSE, KNOWS. Has life ever knocked you so hard that you wondered if you'd be able to get back up? Think about that time now. What knocked you down, and why? What did it take for you to find your feet again? Where did that wellspring of strength come from?

Consider all the struggles that have been faced by those around you. Consider all of the people who have endured challenges and lived to fight another day. You're every bit as resilient as they are.

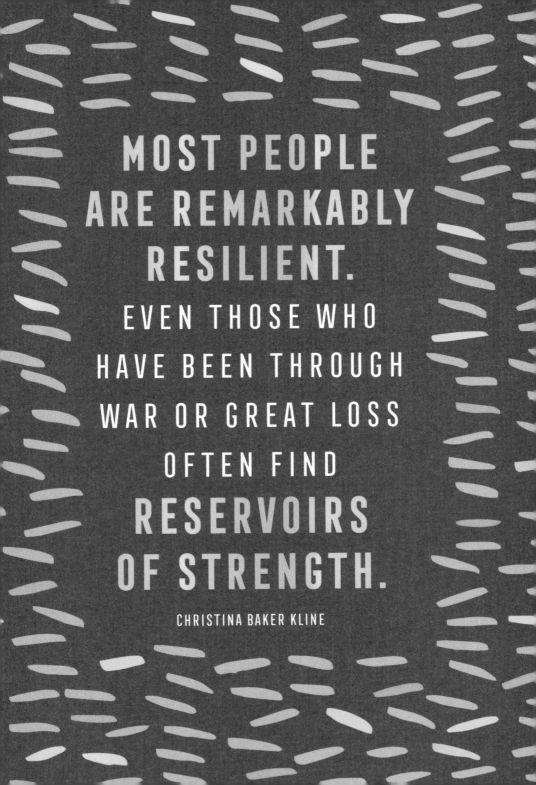

MOST PEOPLE
ARE REMARKABLY
RESILIENT.
EVEN THOSE WHO
HAVE BEEN THROUGH
WAR OR GREAT LOSS
OFTEN FIND
RESERVOIRS
OF STRENGTH.

CHRISTINA BAKER KLINE

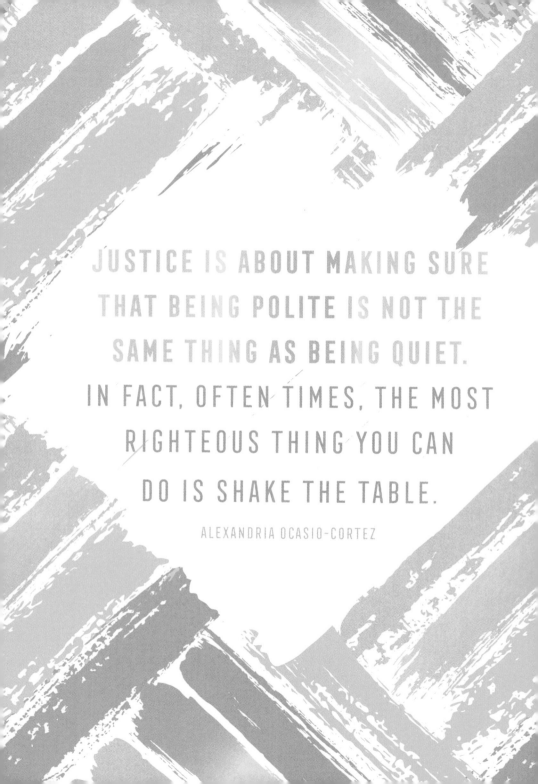

JUSTICE IS ABOUT MAKING SURE
THAT BEING POLITE IS NOT THE
SAME THING AS BEING QUIET.
IN FACT, OFTEN TIMES, THE MOST
RIGHTEOUS THING YOU CAN
DO IS SHAKE THE TABLE.

ALEXANDRIA OCASIO-CORTEZ

BEING NICE shouldn't mean falling in line when we don't want to. Too many times, we succumb to the pressure to be polite and we let our voices be stifled. How much does it matter to you to be well liked? Does it matter too much? What might it cost you?

LET GO OF THE FEELINGS THAT WEIGH YOU DOWN. Be kind to yourself when you feel crushed by others'—and even your own—pessimism and doubt. On days like this, the bravest thing you might do for yourself is to forgive. Forgive those other people. Forgive yourself, too. Remember your gifts. And go in for a reset tomorrow.

If there's someone in your life whom you need to forgive, draft a letter to them here. If you can't bring yourself to send it, consider why that is, and if old grievances or a fear of vulnerability may be weighing down your dreams.

FORGIVENESS
IS A
VIRTUE OF
THE BRAVE.

INDIRA GANDHI

HE WHO
IS BRAVE
IS FREE.

LUCIUS ANNAEUS SENECA

HOW OFTEN do you stop yourself from saying what you really think, or doing what you want to do? Consider these weights that hold you back. Name them here.

Who are you, unencumbered? What would you do with this minute, right now, if you knew you could not fail?

CHALLENGE YOURSELF. Consider that a goal that feels just beyond what you can do may be exactly the right goal to strive for. Can you make your dreams even bigger, more significant? Describe how.

Prod them, challenge them, and be sure you've pushed yourself as far as you can. If you reach a point and say to yourself "that's impossible," stop and challenge that.

THE GREATER DANGER
FOR MOST OF US LIES NOT IN
SETTING OUR AIM TOO HIGH
AND FALLING SHORT;
BUT IN SETTING OUR
AIM TOO LOW, AND
ACHIEVING OUR MARK.

MICHELANGELO

YOU ARE VERY POWERFUL,

PROVIDED YOU KNOW HOW POWERFUL YOU ARE.

YOGI BHAJAN

ONE OF THE MOST IMPORTANT AND UNDERSTATED INGREDIENTS in going for your dreams is realizing you're worth the effort. So cast aside your humility and bask in your own sunshine.

What do you love about being you?

What would you never want to trade about who you are?

If it's hard for you to list things to love about yourself, why do you think that is?

What would your loved ones add to your list?

CONSIDER YOUR MANY INFLUENCES—the people you admire—who are both near to you and strangers. What have they said or done that inspires you? Write a few of their inspirations below—the pieces of them that feel like they're a part of you, too.

Why do you think those particular words or acts resonated so deeply with you?

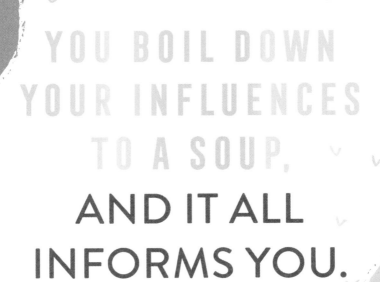

YOU BOIL DOWN YOUR INFLUENCES TO A SOUP, AND IT ALL INFORMS YOU.

JORDAN PEELE

I DON'T THINK ANYONE WHO HAS EVER SPOKEN OUT OR STOOD UP OR HAD A BRAVE MOMENT, HAS REGRETTED IT.

MEGAN RAPINOE

TAKE A WALK DOWN MEMORY LANE and compile a list of your bravest moments. When did you stand up, speak out, and surpass your known capabilities? Dig deep, and ditch modesty.

Remembering who you've been can help to define who you can become.

THOSE WHO GO WHERE NO ONE HAS GONE BEFORE ARE INDEED BRAVE.
These are the people who clear their own way, because no one has forged a path for them. No one has made mistakes and left a guide for doing it right. These people risk mockery, reputations, and livelihoods, and yet they push ahead.

How many pioneers, forerunners, and innovators can you name? How many different forms of bravery can you see in those people? What about each of them reminds you of yourself?

Consider that you are, right now, being asked to clear your own way to a brave new realization about yourself.

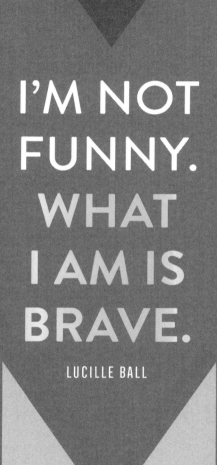

I'M NOT
FUNNY.
WHAT
I AM IS
BRAVE.

LUCILLE BALL

I START OUT WITH
THIS NOTION THAT
I CAN DO ANYTHING.
IT'S NOT UNTIL I GET INTO
IT THAT I REALIZE WHAT I'VE
THROWN MYSELF INTO,
AND THEN I WILL DO
ANYTHING NOT TO
HUMILIATE MYSELF.

MICHELLE PFEIFFER

PRIDE AND EGO are often given a negative connotation, but they can be allies on your way to success. How can you go public with your goal in a way that urges you on? If you put up a billboard proclaiming something to the world, what would it say?

HAVE YOU EVER STOPPED TO ESTIMATE THE LENGTH OF A MINUTE? Set a quiet stopwatch for yourself and close your eyes. Make your guess, then open your eyes to see how you've done. When we pay attention to it, we realize how long a minute can be and how much we can do to fill it.

If you had only a week left to live, what would you do with that time?

Are you a braver person in this *tick-tick-tick* scenario? What feels urgent when you think of last chances? How will you make the most of your minutes?

THE BITTEREST TEARS
SHED OVER GRAVES
ARE FOR WORDS
LEFT UNSAID AND
DEEDS LEFT UNDONE.

HARRIET BEECHER STOWE

GO WITHIN EVERY DAY
AND FIND THE
INNER STRENGTH
SO THAT THE WORLD
WILL NOT BLOW
YOUR CANDLE OUT.

KATHERINE DUNHAM

WHAT INTERNAL SHIFTS would help you to achieve your goals? Give them a score from 1 to 10 to indicate where you believe you are today.

DETERMINATION   1   2   3   4   5   6   7   8   9   10

STAMINA   1   2   3   4   5   6   7   8   9   10

CONFIDENCE   1   2   3   4   5   6   7   8   9   10

Are there actions you might take, even those unrelated to your goals, that might support positive changes within yourself?

Revisit your scores over time, and make note of the quiet changes happening within you. If some scores remain static, dig deep and consider what more you might do to encourage personal growth.

GET BETTER AT RECOGNIZING and then silencing the wrong voices so you can hear the right ones. That your aspirations might be viewed, judged, and commented upon by others can fill your head with worries. If you let them run wild in your mind, they'll weaken your resolve.

Try to judge your worries and reasons dispassionately. Your awareness of them, your study of their fake importance, can make them your new power tools. What are the wrong voices saying?

What are the voices you should be listening to saying?

I LEARNED
THAT COURAGE
WAS NOT THE
ABSENCE OF FEAR,
BUT THE TRIUMPH
OVER IT.

NELSON MANDELA

COURAGE IS CONTAGIOUS.

EVERY TIME WE CHOOSE COURAGE, WE MAKE EVERYONE AROUND US A LITTLE BETTER AND THE WORLD A LITTLE BRAVER.

BRENÉ BROWN

YOU KNOW WHAT YOU WANT, but have you ever considered the greater value of your goals? Bolster them here by naming every good thing that might result from their completion. What is the best possible outcome and how might that lead to other positive outcomes?

How might the changes you make positively impact not only your life, but the lives of others? How might others use your changes to make changes of their own?

GIVING THANKS ISN'T JUST AN ACT OF KINDNESS AND KARMA. Giving thanks for all you have right now, and for each new brave milestone as you reach it, is one of the most reinforcing things you can do for yourself and for others who have supported you. Gratitude isn't only about people, though. Consider places and experiences, too—even objects that you're grateful for, that have made your life better in some way. List them below, and give thanks.

"THANK YOU"

IS THE BEST PRAYER
THAT ANYONE COULD SAY.
I SAY THAT ONE A LOT.

ALICE WALKER

COURAGE IS THE PRICE THAT LIFE EXACTS FOR GRANTING PEACE.

THE SOUL THAT KNOWS IT NOT, KNOWS NO RELEASE FROM LITTLE THINGS; KNOWS NOT THE LIVID LONELINESS OF FEAR; NOR MOUNTAIN HEIGHTS WHERE BITTER JOY CAN HEAR THE SOUND OF WINGS.

AMELIA EARHART

WE ALL WANT THE PEACE that comes from knowing we lived our life to the fullest. Search your mind. What change would assure you that you did not sell yourself short and that you lived life right?

Change requires action. And action requires movement, and often the clang and clatter of a relentless voice. What actions on your part are the key to that sense of peace?

CONSIDER HOW YOU'VE LIVED YOUR LIFE UP TO THIS POINT. If you had a mantra up until now, what would it be?

Now give it a chiropractic adjustment to make it braver. What is your new mantra?

MY MANTRA HAS ALWAYS BEEN TO HAVE ZERO REGRETS IN LIFE. EVERYTHING I DO AT ONE SPEED, I GO ALL-OUT.

APOLO OHNO

THE ONLY THING
TO DO WITH
GOOD ADVICE
IS TO PASS IT ON.
IT IS NEVER OF ANY
USE TO ONESELF.

OSCAR WILDE

AS YOU JOURNEY TO YOUR GOALS, you will undoubtedly learn a lot about yourself, but also about life. You'll grow wiser with every milestone. With whom will you share these pearls?

Who in your life has shared their learned wisdom with you? How has their journey resembled your own?

REJECT THE LURE OF THE EASY ROUTE—the route of quitting, of giving up, of settling. Write yourself a note right now, for that future moment when it feels too hard, and you're on the edge of living a safer life—one that doesn't move you out of your comfort zone. Remind yourself why the struggle is worthwhile. Reach out to your future self who is letting the fire burn out, and rouse her passion again.

NEVER GIVE UP,

FOR THAT IS JUST THE PLACE AND TIME THAT THE TIDE WILL TURN.

HARRIET BEECHER STOWE

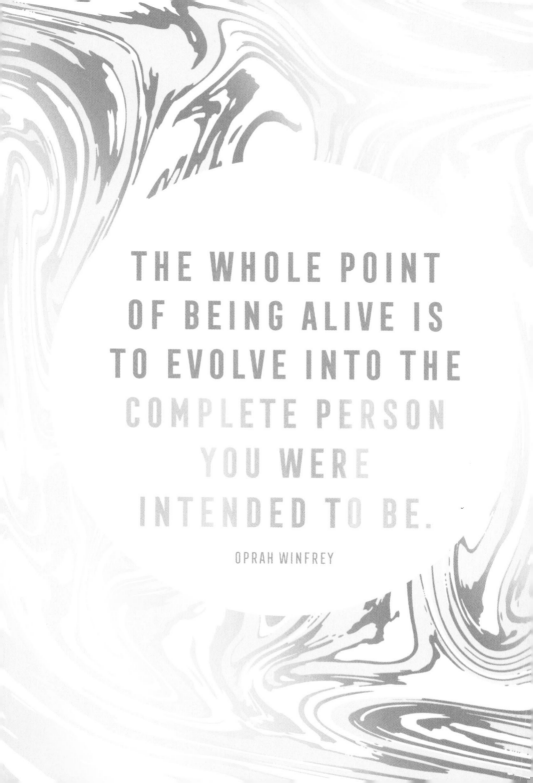

THE WHOLE POINT
OF BEING ALIVE IS
TO EVOLVE INTO THE
COMPLETE PERSON
YOU WERE
INTENDED TO BE.

OPRAH WINFREY

THE DREAM OF SELF-ACTUALIZATION IS INSPIRING. Imagine living your bravest life as the years and decades pass. How do you change? What new dreams might you imagine next? How does brave look on you?

At the pinnacle, who might you become? What does your voice sound like, and what might you holler to the world? What is your legacy?

BRAVE ACTS   DATE

DARING GOALS   DATE ACHIEVED